IMAGES
of America

COLORADO
NATIONAL MONUMENT

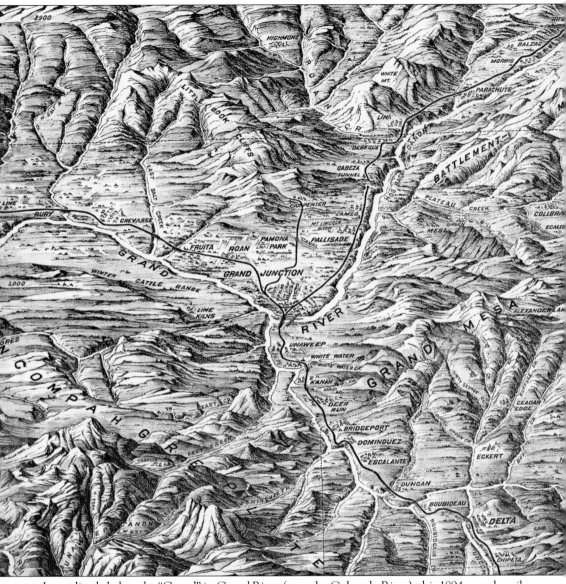

Immediately below the "Grand" in Grand River (now the Colorado River), this 1894 map describes the land once used as "Winter Cattle Range" but is now managed by the Colorado National Monument. East across the valley, the "Grand Mesa" flat-topped mountain was once considered a component in a plan to combine both areas into a national park. (Cartography by Frank Pezolt; courtesy of the U.S. Geological Survey.)

ON THE COVER: John Otto was the Colorado National Monument's first custodian, trail builder, horseman, promoter, and self-professed "World's Greatest Radical of the Safe Kind." With a system of trails he personally built, Otto provided access along the sheer rock walls and monoliths of the beautifully desolate red-rock canyons. One of the most challenging trails was appropriately named the Corkscrew Trail from the Liberty Cap down approximately 500 vertical feet to the canyon floor. (Courtesy of the National Park Service.)

IMAGES
of America

COLORADO
NATIONAL MONUMENT

Alan J. Kania

ARCADIA
PUBLISHING

Published by Arcadia Publishing
Charleston, South Carolina

Printed in the United States of America

Library of Congress Catalog Card Number: 2008933331

For all general information contact Arcadia Publishing at:
Telephone 843-853-2070
Fax 843-853-0044
E-mail sales@arcadiapublishing.com
For customer service and orders:
Toll-Free 1-888-313-2665

Visit us on the Internet at www.arcadiapublishing.com

Dedicated to the friends of the
Colorado National Monument Association
and seasonal park rangers and volunteers
through the U.S. National Park Service

CONTENTS

ACKNOWLEDGMENTS

My parents, Frank and Genevieve Kania, justified family clutter in simple terms: "If you don't have to feed it, keep it." It is that philosophy that prompts my gratitude to the families who opened their family photo albums and scrapbooks to create this tribute to their ancestors and to the Colorado National Monument. A tip of John Otto's broad-brimmed hat goes to the families Benge, Chester, Ela, and Otto.

A great deal of gratitude goes to the archivists at the National Archives and Records Administration, Denver Federal Center, for being so efficient in helping me sift through the National Park Service files.

I am always envious when I deal with the National Park Service. These are the people who live the stories about which I can only write. Special thanks to Denise Hight, manager of the Colorado National Monument Association, and her husband, Steve, for their assistance in gaining access to the park photographs. Thanks also to Michelle Wheatley (park ranger supervisor/education coordinator), Dave Price (chief resource management), Annie Williams (interpretive park ranger) and Hank Schoch (chief ranger, retired) for locating other Colorado National Monument photographs and verifying some of the information used to identify them.

Many of the Colorado National Monument and Civilian Conservation Corps (CCC) camp pictures are in the repository of the National Park Service's Western Archeological and Conservation Center. Particular thanks to archivist Lynn Marie Mitchell, Khaleel Saba (assistant archivist), and Kristi Ausfresser (archives technician).

And as always, appreciation goes to the stalwarts of the Colorado archives that I used in completing this book—the Museum of Western Colorado (Michael Menard, curator of archives/ library), Colorado State Archives, Denver Public Library's Western History Department, National Park Service archives, and the State Historical Society of Colorado.

I also wish to thank my editors at Arcadia Publishing, Hannah Carney and Jerry Roberts, for their expert guidance and great senses of humor. And to Arcadia author Barbara Proko, who encouraged me to pursue this project.

And many thanks to my wife, Terry, for her patience, guidance, and love during the research, writing, and production of this book.

INTRODUCTION

Walter Walker, editor of the *Grand Junction Daily Sentinel*, published the following in the *Denver Times* on October 9, 1910.

Among the quaint and picturesque characters of the present day West, among those men of the "land of the sky," who furnish to the curious extraordinary opportunities for character study, there is today, on the sunny western slope of Colorado, where mighty mountains reach down and touch fruit-laden valleys, a strange embodiment of rare human qualities known as John Otto, trail builder, trapper, hermit, scout, cowboy and philosopher.

The work this man has done, the sacrifices he has made, the wonders of physical exertion he has performed are beginning to attract national note. Born in Missouri thirty-eight years ago, the member of a cultured family, son of a man who today holds the chair of languages in a great Eastern educational institution, John Otto wandered from home more than twenty years ago, drifted West, roamed from the Rocky mountains to the Pacific, and finally found himself back among the Rockies working as a cowboy. All who met him liked him. He seemed ever to be trying to do something to lighten the burden and to increase the happiness of his fellow men.

One day, some four years ago, a tall, black haired, handsome, lithe young man appeared in Grand Junction, Colo., the thriving modern little city in the midst of the famous Grand valley fruit section, and declared that to the west and south of that city just a few miles, there lay a series of canons, gorges, peaks, etc. that made up a wonderful territory. Oldtimers laughed at the young fellow, ridiculed his idea of a section that had heretofore been regarded simply as a roving place for stray cattle, and as inaccessible to travelers. The young man was John Otto. He accepted the ridicule in silence. He secured some meager supplies, packed them on his burros and was gone again.

Before a great while reports began to drift to the city to the effect that this strange young man was at work trying to build trails along the mountainsides and bordering the gorges of what was commonly known as the Monument park country. The reports would be greeted with laughter. The months passed. Occasionally this man would come to town, secure supplies and return to the mountain haunts.

One day a traveler returning from a trip to the Monument park section, startled the citizens with a story to the effect that he had found a mile or two of remarkable trail skirting a mountainside, built by John Otto, and that Otto was constructing more trail. The Chamber of Commerce appointed a committee to investigate, the trip was made and when the committee returned the tales it told were like unto those related by the spies sent by the children of Israel to view the promised land of Canaan.

Beyond the skyline of those peaks and granite walls they found that John Otto had discovered a mighty paradise of natural beauty that, bent upon opening this lovely wilderness to man's footsteps he had, without aid and without the hope or chance of personal gain, constructed long stretches of most difficult and wonderful trails. The report of the committee created a sensation. No longer was Otto regarded as being stupid, but by many was looked upon as being extremely foolish for putting all his energies into a herculean task when he had nothing personally to gain.

From that time on parties began to make excursions to Monument park and each time new facts concerning the beauty of the canons and the wonderful nature of the trail were learned.

But the strange man of the mountains gave but little heed to the wondering people. He kept on at work. Occasionally he came to town with a burro or two, would give a few citizens an opportunity to contribute a dollar each to a fund to buy powder for blasting and other supplies, never asking for more than $1 and never approaching the same person twice. He wanted nothing for his labor and would accept nothing. All funds contributed were spent on the trail. When he needed money for clothing, etc., he would go to some ranch, work a few days or a few weeks and earn sufficient for his needs.

Investigation of the paradise of natural beauty Otto was opening to the world revealed a series of immense and lovely canons, scores of might "monuments" or rocks shooting up from canon floor to distances of from seventy to 550 feet, spacious caves, waterfalls, grassy dells, wooded mountain sides and many fantastic and peculiar natural formations. Appreciating the loveliness and grandeur of this wild and rugged section so long regarded as hopelessly inaccessible, John Otto had conceived the idea of conquering those perilous and extensive canon walls and mountains with a trail, and to himself he dedicated the great task and, to use his own language, "set in to make that big territory of use to man and for his pleasure."

Today, some four years after he started work on Trail No. 1, the sightseer who visits the domain of John Otto stands amazed and unbelieving when he finds that over nine miles of difficult mountain trails have been built by this one man without help of another human hand and with financial aid aggregating not more than $250—a series of trails that had it been built by any county or city would have cost not less than $20,000 for labor alone.

Trail No. 1 is five miles in length and Trail No. 2 is over four miles in length. In the construction of both trails surveying and engineering feats of greatest difficulty were encountered, yet this man solved them all, and today these trails, climbing perilous heights, skirting deep gorges, passing under mighty cliffs, ascend at an easy grade from the valley level to an altitude of some 8,000 feet, affording views of unsurpassed beauty and making an entrance easy for man and beast into a fairyland of natural masterpieces.

Day in and day out for years this lone man worked on these trails. He mourned if he lost a day. He worked early and late. When the snows came he would shovel it from the right of way and continue work. His physical endurance is the marvel of all, and how he accomplished many of the titanic features of the work is hard to comprehend. For hundreds of yards the trails are literally blasted out of steep cliffs of solid granite: in other places great timbers would have to be dragged up canon walls and put in shape to hold the trail in place against the precipice. Yet one man did it all. He moved his camping outfit along the trail as he progressed.

The trails became known as Otto's trails, and then it was found that this strange being had named all the canons and "monuments," and on many he had engraved inscriptions. Every name had its significance, easily explained and easily understood. Among the canons are Shackelton, Red, Half Moon, Horseshoe, No Thoroughfare and many others.

When he named the vast array of "monuments" which really stand as true wonders of the Rockies, owing to their enormous height and marvelous formation, he delved into American history and selected names from the roster of the great men of the past. On one great rock he inscribed the names of the signers of the Declaration of Independence and called it Independence monument.

High above them all, a veritable monument on a monument is a temple-like formation which he calls "Temple Monument," and declares that it stands as an inspiration from God and Heaven, and an indication of man's insignificance.

People who continued skeptical declared that in the summer there would be no permanent water supply. Otto broke down this contention by the discovery at various points along the trail and in the canons of everlasting springs. He gave each of these symbolic or significant names, among them being Evergreen, Purity, Good Luck, Butterfly, Lone Cottonwood and others. At [E]vergreen Springs, the first encountered along the trail, in a stone vault, he keeps the registration book wherein are subscribed the names of those who contributed to the trail fund.

The anniversaries of birthdays of great men or patriotic anniversaries have been celebrated by Otto in an extraordinary manner. Frequently he has hauled or packed to high points on the mountains load after load of firewood and on the evening of the anniversary would light a great beacon fire which could be seen for miles and miles and which always attracts the attention of thousands of people.

Otto announced this year that on July 4th, he would unfurl on the top of one of the towering "monuments," an American flag. The walls of the mighty rock are as perpendicular and smooth as the walls of a smoke stack, reaching up to a height of over 400 feet, with a diameter at the base of about seventy feet and of about twenty at the top. Yet this man took his life in his hands, drilled hole after hole in the rock, drove in spikes and step after step in this manner, after days and days of work, he reached the summit, placed a pole in a drilled hole, arranged pulleys, descended in safety and on July 4th, in the presence of many people he unfurled a big flag which still proudly waves high above the Grand valley.

Otto's domain is all government land. His discoveries and explorations and his wonderful work attracted the attention of the forest reserve and to its officials he pointed out many advantages. Then Otto not only planned but carried out a plan to open, by the means of his trail, a mode of passage into the Big Park country, a rich agricultural section, and this was quickly peopled by settlers. He then began to talk about preserving his domain to posterity as a national park. He wrote to President Taft[;] the chief executive was interested and replied. On his trip through the West in the fall of 1909 he met and greeted Otto at Grand Junction.

The governor of Colorado became interested and had a conference with Otto. Then in the United States senate and in the lower house bills making Monument park a national park and setting aside some 25,000 acres of land for the same, were introduced and are certain to get through at the coming session, there being no opposition.

The Monument park promises to become one of the scenic and pleasure-breeding wonders of the West. All because of the efforts of this strange man Otto [who] is by no means ignorant. He keeps in touch with all the big events of the day, can discuss the tariff as fluently as he can talk of a mountain trail. He is a retiring sort of fellow, avoids notoriety and the accompanying photograph is the only one he has ever consented to have made. He is as poor today as the day he began his herculean task. He is today at work on more trails in the canons. He never remains away from the mountain fastnesses any longer than necessary. He lives alone far up among the crags in winter and summer, and in all the great West no more interesting, quaint or picturesque character can be found than this true noble man of the royal Court of Nature.

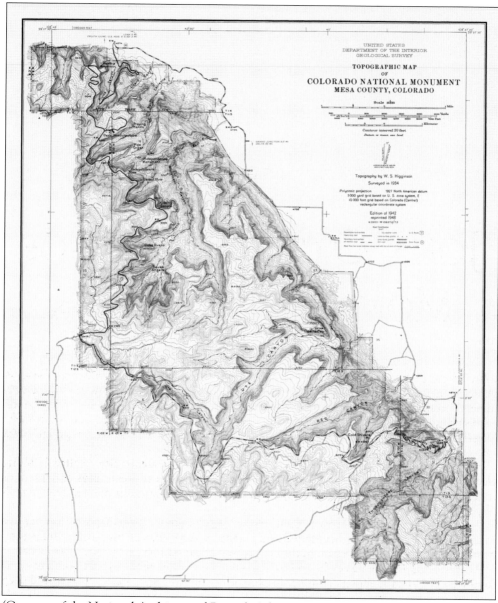

(Courtesy of the National Archives and Records Administration, Denver.)

One

JOHN OTTO, HERMIT OF MONUMENT CANYON

John Otto took his progressive upbringing to heart as he traveled throughout the West. A voracious newspaper reader, John followed the unsafe conditions and 12-hour working days miners experienced in tunnel mining. When women were seeking access to the voting booth, John supported their equality. And when the advent of the automobile spurred motorists to make long-distance sojourns, he proposed incorporating the newly established system of national parks into cross-country highway system.

His flamboyant way of promoting his points of view often threatened elected officials during election campaigns. To keep Otto out of the press, he was arrested three times as a threat to state governors. Only one of his "insanity trials" resulted in a brief incarceration in an asylum in Napa County, California.

When he was released and ultimately settled near Grand Junction, Colorado, he took great pride in challenging the sanity of other Mesa County residents. After all, with his certificate of release, he boasted he was the only person in the county who could actually prove that he was sane.

After working as a laborer on the Fruita (Colorado) Water Pipeline through the scenic canyons southwest of Grand Junction, Otto began promoting the red rocks, majestic spires, and deep canyons. Most residents considered the canyons to be inaccessible box canyons where local cattle ranchers could winter their livestock.

Otto built a series of sophisticated trails that crossed geological uplifts and picked their way along rock walls. With the support of the Grand Junction and Fruita Chambers of Commerce and the editor of the *Daily Sentinel*, county residents began to appreciate the beauty of the canyons. So successful was their marketing campaign that U.S. president William Taft added the Colorado National Monument to the U.S. National Park Service on May 24, 1911. Because of his dedication to the canyons, Otto was named the first custodian of the Colorado National Monument for a salary of $1 a month. A series of arguments about the location of a coast-to-coast highway that bypassed the monument in the late 1920s resulted in Otto's departure for Northern California in the early 1930s.

© Colorado Historical Society

Tried three times for insanity (and found sane on each occasion), accused of attempting to assassinate the governor of Colorado (and later exonerated), and often dressed in a green shirt with colored stars for buttons, John Otto became the Colorado National Monument's first custodian and most ardent booster. His prankish sense of humor once prompted him to propose renaming the monument "Smith National Park" (the commercial possibilities were "stupendous," he wrote). An early women's advocate, he was married briefly and later awarded alimony from the bride who deserted him. When he was not writing rambling letters-to-the-editor for local newspapers on current events, he single-handedly built trails in the Colorado National Monument. He was an avid proponent of expanding the park to include the entire Grand Valley around Grand Junction to the Utah border as one of many national parks united by his proposed national park highway system. (Courtesy of the State Historical Society of Colorado.)

Insane Asylum, Napa, Cal.

While working as an itinerant farm laborer, John Otto questioned why people did not volunteer their services for the betterment of their community. He believed volunteerism was "Better than Money." He was so passionate about his credo that townspeople thought he had the potential of becoming violent. California gubernatorial candidate George Pardee became alarmed when Otto's rants interfered with Pardee's campaign. He made sure Otto was kept incommunicado in the Napa State Hospital for the insane until after the election. "The Castle" maintained a "backyard" where the men could socialize. Fruit orchards, available so men could learn an agricultural trade, grew on the opposite side of the back wall. (Both, courtesy of the Napa State Hospital.)

PICTURE TAKEN OF OTTO WHILE MINING IN WASHINGTON

OTTO'S CABIN WHILE MINING.

After being released from Napa State Hospital, John moved to Colorado, where he became an advocate of the eight-hour workday for miners. When he aggressively sought an audience with Gov. James Peabody, the Pinkerton Detective Agency lay in wait in the governor's vacated office. (Courtesy of the *Denver Republican*.)

In an interview with the local newspapers, Otto explained he did not mean to harm the governor but only to advise him on the local labor issues on behalf of the Colorado miners. His discourse became animated, and he proposed all members of the legislature be brought before the "Great Grand Jury" for not passing the eight-hour law. (Courtesy of the *Rocky Mountain News*.)

MINER WHO THREATENED GOVERNOR PROVES TO BE HARMLESS CRANK

John Otto, Originally Charged With "Attempt to Assault," Will Be Subjected to Insanity Inquisition Inasmuch as He Exhibits at County Jail Unmistakable Signs of Mental Unbalance —Claims He Has Solution of Labor Problem.

JOHN OTTO,
Socialist Who Gave Governor Bad Scare.

JOHN OTTO BEING TAKEN FROM THE STATE HOUSE TO THE COUNTY JAIL BY UNDERSHERIFF O'NEILL, DEPUTY DE LUE AND PINKERTON AGENT PRETTYMAN.

Undersheriff O'Neill, Deputy deLue, and Pinkerton Agent J. J. Prettyman led John Otto (third from left wearing the "darbies" handcuffs) away from the Colorado State Capitol in Denver. The officers found a miner's candlestick in Otto's pocket and erroneously feared it could have been used as a "stiletto-shaped weapon" against the governor. (Courtesy of the *Denver Post*.)

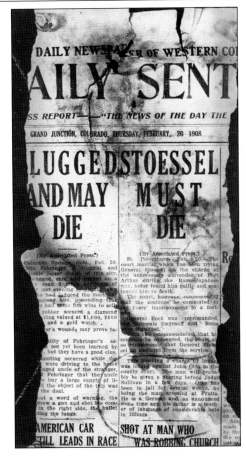

Many years later, a can attached to a long rope was found hanging over the edge of the canyon walls of the Colorado National Monument. Enclosed was a newspaper clipped describing Otto's third insanity trial, this time involving comments made to Colorado governor Henry A. Buchtel. Attached to the canister was a handwritten note: "FALSEHOOD!" (Courtesy of the National Park Service.)

Artifacts associated with the Folsom and Yuma cultures (from 25,000 to 10,000 BC) have been found in the area around Grand Junction, Colorado. It was not until the Basket Maker II and III agricultural culture (post-300 AD) that archeologists could verify the first residents of the Grand Valley. Artifacts from the Pueblos (from 700 to 1600 AD) were also found in the area. Padre Escalante and the Dominguez expedition of 1776 probably met with the Ute Indians, who resided in the Colorado National Monument area until settlers arriving in 1881 sent them to reservations. (Both, courtesy of the National Park Service.)

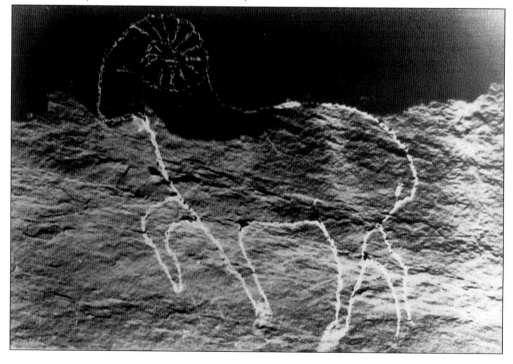

From the top of Riggs Hill, the steep cliffs of the western portion of the Colorado River can be seen beyond the farmland and orchards of what is described as the Redlands of Grand Junction, Colorado. Before the Colorado National Monument was established as part of the National Park Service, the land against the cliffs was used for livestock. (Courtesy of National Archives and Record Center, Denver.)

On the western side of Fruita Canyon, livestock operators used stock driveways to move livestock from the Glade Park region above the Colorado National Monument to their winter grazing area on the valley floor. John Otto often fought the ranchers because the ranchers occasionally utilized his trails as stock driveways. (Courtesy of the National Park Service.)

Colorado winter grazing land gradually became farms and orchards along the foothills of the Colorado National Monument. The main entrance to Independence Monument (the right portion of the photograph) brought tourists to the 500-foot monolith and a canyon with other rock features. Encouragement from the competing Fruita and Grand Junction Chambers of Commerce and the

residents of Glade Park prompted John Otto to build additional access points at No Thoroughfare Canyon on the eastern side of the monument and Fruita Canyon on the western side to provide more direct access to the rim rocks of the monument. (Photograph by Dean Studios; courtesy of the author's collection.)

While John Otto built trails along the eastern borders of what would become Trail No. 1 in the Colorado National Monument, he attracted the attention of the business community in Grand Junction and Fruita. The trail is located west of the Devil's Kitchen in No Thoroughfare Canyon, the closest access point from Grand Junction. Even day hikers used burros to pack picnic lunches for large groups. Otto took great pride in showing the marketing potential of the canyons located between the two communities. In the line of well-dressed hikers, John Otto stands third from the left. (Both, courtesy of the author's collection.)

John Otto's trails traversed bare rock as they gained altitude from the valley floor. To weather horse and foot traffic, Otto (sixth hiker in line) drilled holes and concreted metal pipes into the sandstone rock. He used slash timber along the pipes and leveled the trail with gravel. Evidence of some of the original trails is still visible a century later. (Courtesy of the author's collection.)

Below the monoliths John Otto named after presidents, a line of hikers (bottom center of the picture) travel along Trail No. 1. The large monolith at the center of the picture is the Jefferson Memorial, and the three smaller monoliths to the right were named after the three martyred presidents—Lincoln, Garfield, and McKinley. (Courtesy of the author's collection.)

The Grand Junction newspaper recognized that the agricultural community of Glade Park was linked to the railroad in Grand Junction by "the merest excuse for a trail. . . . A good road should be constructed into it at once and if the county commissioners cannot do it . . . the road should be built by private citizens." John Otto saw an opportunity to expand his system of trails into a wagon road across the eastern portion of what would become the Colorado National Monument. From horseback and on foot, he began to design the roadway. (Above, courtesy of the State Historical Society of Colorado; below, courtesy of the Chester family.)

In 1908, John Otto remarked, "A natural monument high and grand, stands in front of the red rim on the granite bench, and I hope you will agree with me in naming it the Jefferson Monument in honor of the author of the Declaration of Independence, of the famous bill for religious freedom in Virginia, patriot, president and American." (Courtesy of the author's collection.)

At the base of Jefferson Monument, John Otto (with shovel) used a gold-painted pick and shovel to open a new section of his trail across the face of the monument. With him stand the executive committee members of the Grand Junction Chamber of Commerce. The trail implements were then put on display in the window of the Fair Store to help publicize Otto's trail-building efforts. (Courtesy of the author's collection.)

John Otto never missed an opportunity to publicize the Colorado National Monument. Photographers from the local newspapers, chambers of commerce, railroad destination magazines, and other promotional periodicals could easily draw Otto from his trail work and into his secondary responsibility as tour guide. In the picture below, Otto is seated in the middle of the group of well-dressed hikers posed at the entrance of Monument Canyon. Independence Monument is silhouetted against the skyline. (Left, courtesy of the National Park Service; below, courtesy of the Chester family.)

While community leaders sought a name for the national parkland, the *Daily Sentinel* suggested naming it "Smith National Monument Park." The author (presumably John Otto) noted there were more Smiths than Joneses living in the Grand Valley area. A "Smith National Monument Association" could be responsible for organizing annual Smith family reunions, bringing millions of Smiths to the national park that bore their surname. Since the author claimed the relations would spend an average of two weeks each year at the monument, he computed that $20 million could be spent each year at the reunions. (Courtesy of the State Historical Society of Colorado.)

At the top of the Corkscrew Trail, a large haystack-like mound of sandstone greeted hikers. Grand Junction Chamber of Commerce president Thomas F. Mahony had the honor of naming the formation. John Otto bore a hole on top and proposed to fly an American flag on the Fourth of July in 1909. (Courtesy of the author's collection.)

Prior to the establishment of the national monument in 1911, a list of potential names for the park was discussed. The naming rights went to Mrs. Edward T. Taylor, wife of the U.S. representative who made the formal application to create the Colorado National Monument. Representative Taylor also made an appropriation of $25,000 for John Otto to build his self-designed road into the monument. (Courtesy of the Chester family.)

John Otto (right) was once urged to move into Fruita or Grand Junction, where he could live in a more civilized apartment. His response was, "I live in a tent and pay no rent." He moved his base camp as he advanced construction on the trails. Later U.S. Census Bureau reports indicated he did trade his trail camps for apartment life in town. (Courtesy of the National Park Service.)

Rowdy, Otto's favorite horse, was shared with visitors for special occasions. As he reported to the newspaper, "Miss Bertha Schwartz, daughter of Mr. Wm. Schwartz, the spud king of Fruita and Miss Lillian Weckel, a popular teacher of Grand Junction, rode on 'Rowdy' clear to the top [of Liberty Cap]; the first lady to ride a horse over the new trail." (Courtesy of the Chester family.)

Enos A. Mills, a Rocky Mountain naturalist, endorsed John Otto's (mounted on horseback) trail plan: "I will not overlook the opportunity to make Monument Canyon the subject of magazine articles. There is no reason why from 2,000 to 3,000 tourists should not visit this city every year to see [the monument] . . . and it is certain that many will leave money here in substantial investments." (Left, courtesy of the State Historical Society of Colorado; below, courtesy of the National Park Service.)

Mills continued, "A good road to Monument canon would be as useful as an irrigation ditch through an acre of desert. Three or four miles of trails would make all the points of interest accessible and John Otto will build that with little money and little help." (Above, courtesy of the National Park Service; below, courtesy of the State Historical Society of Colorado.)

When John Otto was not building trails, he took time off to explore other "monuments," canyons, and rock arches between the park and Utah borders. He believed the western land (now managed by the Bureau of Land Management) could expand the geological scope of the Colorado National Monument. (Courtesy of the Museum of Western Colorado.)

Otto (standing and facing left with broad-brimmed hat) provided comfortable amenities for his trail guests. Rest spots were often incorporated along the trail. If shade trees were not naturally available, he planted fruit trees and turned small trickles of spring water into catch basins for the benefit of pack animals and hikers. (Courtesy of the author's collection.)

To try and contain the wildlife within the Colorado National Monument, Otto utilized dead timber and unrolled wire-mesh animal fencing across the canyons. The canyons that provided natural enclosures for the winter-grazing livestock became natural walls for Otto's attempt at creating a wildlife sanctuary. (Courtesy of the National Park Service.)

Record books were stashed throughout the park. Otto encouraged people to sign and register their comments about the park. The Cave of Records, located near the Liberty Cap above the Corkscrew Trail, was supposed to be the permanent repository of the record books. (Courtesy of the State Historical Society of Colorado.)

Without a formal background of civil engineering, John Otto plotted his plans for a trail and road system to connect the scenic highlights of the Grand Valley. On a photograph, Otto proposed American flags on Mounts Garfield and Lincoln in the Little Bookcliffs north of the valley and a trail that continued south to the palisades below Grand Mesa, east of the valley. (Courtesy of the Chester family.)

Grand Junction historian and newspaper advertising man Al Look examines the monument Otto had made in response to Otto's visit to the Panama-Pacific International Exposition. The reverse swastika, a part of the history of the American Indian as well as other cultures throughout the world, created a misunderstanding among Grand Junction servicemen during World War II. (Courtesy of the Colorado National Monument.)

While Otto was striving for national attention for his Colorado National Monument project, he invited U.S. president William Taft to personally visit the park; Taft initially turned down the invitation. With a little persistence on Otto's part, Taft eventually did accept the invitation to come accept bushels of Grand Valley fruit and to meet the Palisade Peach Queen. In return, the chief executive sent an American flag that Otto flew from Independence Monument. "It is not my flag," wrote Otto to the *Daily Sentinel*, "as far as ownership is concerned; I am just caring for it; it is everybody's flag." (Both, courtesy of the State Historical Society of Colorado.)

As evidenced by rock graffiti from 1837, Antonio Robideaux was the first European man to pass through the Grand Valley. The Grand Junction Chamber of Commerce asked President Taft to name the park project after the explorer, but a more generic name was selected. (Courtesy of the National Park Service.)

While Otto served as custodian of the monument, the Grand Junction Chamber of Commerce provided office space for the trail builder. During the most acerbic period between John Otto and W. M. "Woody" Wood, secretary of the business organization, the two men wrote critical letters about each other from adjoining offices at the chamber office without ever speaking to each other. (Courtesy of the author's collection.)

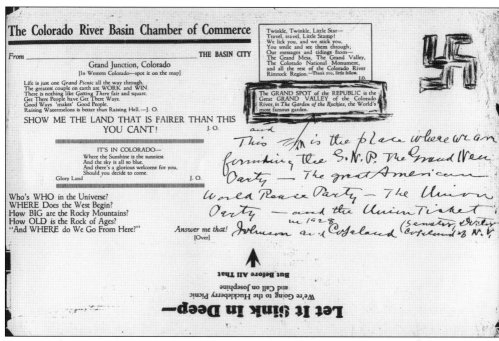

In 1927, John wavered as to whether he wanted to continue his decade as custodian. He told the National Park Service he began the Colorado River Basin Chamber of Commerce. His letterhead and envelopes left little room for an address or message. Otto's propensity for social-political poetry, catch phrases, and literary monologues boosted the scenic beauties more flamboyantly than any chamber of commerce. When he used the stationery to promote the G.N.P.—Grand New Party—the park service deemed Otto was venturing into politics and terminated his $1 a month job as custodian of the Colorado National Monument. (Both, courtesy of the Chester family.)

John Otto had several dogs as his trailside companions. He attempted to get one of his dogs to "look at the camera" while posed in front of the popular rock formation in No Thoroughfare Canyon near the bottom of the Trail of the Serpent. One of his dogs had the tragic habit of barking at lit dynamite fuses, usually backing off before the detonation occurred. Otto's next dog was kept away from the sparking fuses. The rock amphitheater was previously called Castle Rock; during Arbor Day, it was renamed King Apple's Castle. With the serpent and apple connotations, the rock formation became known as the Devil's Kitchen. (Courtesy of the author's collection.)

Two

A WEDDING OF
INDEPENDENCE

In a series of letters-to-the-editor published in 1911 editions of the *Daily Sentinel* newspaper, John Otto expressed his opinion of marriage. The wedding of Otto and Massachusetts artist Beatrice Farnham was as controversial as the bride and groom.

To all its Friends and the Public at Large," began John Otto, "It is well known, that the Monument park is a big proposition, soon to be permanently established as a playground for all people. For over two years I have spent time and money on nothing but public domain, simply taking a chance that the Monument and the adjoining canyons would be combined into one grand park; have worked alone for a long time, but now am alone no more. The other day "my partner" arrived, Miss Beatrice Farnham, artist, trail girl of the Southwest. I sincerely believe I have pursued my labors honorably over here in these hills and, now as there are two, we assure the *Sentinel*, that work will be continued on the same basis.

To make a long story short, we announce our engagement, to be married after the flag raising on the Independence tower in June. As to details, it's simply 'the story of the guide, who couldn't be hired.'

. . . Marriage is all foolishness. . . . I don't believe in the modern form of marriage. It isn't formed on common sense. I am doing it, not because I believe in the modern marriage system, but because I believe in obeying the law of the land, no matter what it is. The law provides that a man shall marry according to certain forms, that he gets a marriage license and have an authorized person officiate at the wedding, and I want to obey the law in every respect. . . . Marriage can only be founded on love, and it's silly to try to read into the ceremony to 'honor and obey.' I never heard of a woman obeying—her husband, anyway—and what is the use of making them lie every time they stand up before a minister? If the present marriage system was right, we wouldn't have all these divorces.

. . . We are not seeking notoriety and hate 'scenes.' We have both agreed to the one thing— we want to be married 'outdoors . . . in the blessed outdoors . . . out in the big country.'

mrs. Otto

"Western men like intelligent women," Beatrice Farnham, an artist from South Weymouth, Massachusetts, explained. "I mean real women—women who haven't time for foolishness. Western men don't care for Eastern dolls with empty brains. They admire, respect and love the women alert and vigorous, ready to fashion her own life without help from anybody else." (Photograph by Whipple Chester; courtesy of the Ela family.)

John Otto said, "In good, plain, straight, easy, understandable words: It is all a D— lie that I 'had hoped to be wed on top of Independence and had driven pegs in the sides for the ascent.' That's all mighty punk publicity to say such stuff." (Photograph by Whipple Chester; courtesy of Daniel Otto Schmid.)

John Otto

The Episcopal liturgy for the Otto-Farnham wedding was conducted by the Reverend F. A. Hatch, pastor of the Congregational church in Fruita. Beatrice wore a white satin dress with a veil and scarf originally worn by her grandmother 70 years ago. The bouquet was comprised of Colorado wildflowers. On a quartz ledge in the shadow of Temple Rock, Otto told his best man, Whipple Chester, the bride and groom would "mount a high promontory beyond the eyes of other humans and plight their troth before God and the Stars and Stripes in their own peculiar, yet even more beautiful and sincere way." (Photographs by Whipple Chester; courtesy of the Ela family.)

The wedding in Monolith National Park. John Otto

The Otto-Farnham prenuptial feast, prepared by the bride over a campfire, included tomato soup, roasted chicken, boiled tongue, salads, bread, preserves, coffee, lemonade, and other delights, served in the shade of a large pinion tree in Monument Canyon. Rev. F. A. Hatch provided the grace. (Photograph by Whipple Chester; courtesy of the National Park Service.)

John Otto (left) and an associate scaled Independence Monument prior to the wedding and hammered metal pipes into the sheer rock monolith. The local newspaper speculated that Otto's intentions were to hold the wedding ceremony at the summit, a story he emphatically denied. (Photograph by Whipple Chester; courtesy of the National Park Service.)

Mid-1970s Colorado National Monument superintendent Robert Benton (left) and a visiting National Park Service rock climber hold the twisted remains of one of John Otto's flagpoles, which was discarded off the top of Independence Monument. Park rangers found the connected pipes at the base of the monolith. (Courtesy of the National Park Service.)

While John hung 500 feet above on the rock face, he asked Beatrice to carve the last sentence of the Declaration of Independence onto a large slab of rock that had fallen. "I am greatly impressed with the scheme," wrote Beatrice. "I shall cut the letters out one by one and fill the hollows with white cement, which will contrast prettily with the dark red stone." (Courtesy of the National Park Service.)

Beatrice Farnham Paints Picture of Otto as He Picks Way to top of Monument

With her lover, John Otto, perched on a steel pipe five hundred feet above her, drilling his way to the top of Independence Tower in Monument Canon, Miss Beatrice Farnham of South Weymouth, Mass., artist and nature lover, sits far below painting a picture of the titantic pile of perpendicular stone, which her fiance is trying to scale. From where she sits she can see him with his drill and hammer working relentlessly, patiently to conquer the gigantic monolith which has never been scaled by man.

He drills for an hour or so on one hole every moment in danger of being blown from his perch or of losing his balance. The hole bored to the required depth a piece of steel pipe is wedged in and he climbs one peg higher to start a new hole in the rock wall.

From the canon below the form of Otto clinging to the cliff is almost invisible and looks like a tiny piece of cloth or inanimate object, as no movement can be discerned, except when he climbs up or down. The

fact that John Otto is hourly in peril does not seem to worry Miss Farnham, who has implicit faith in his ability to accomplish the work safely. She enjoys her painting and sings softly as she adds touches of color to the canvas, which promises to be a rare picture of the great stone tower.

Miss Farnham's camp, close to John Otto's regular Monument canon camp, 13 miles west of this city. She expects to remain there all summer obtaining views of the canon.

For an engagement present, John Otto gave Beatrice Farnham a pack burro. "While I can't wear it," she explained, "it will come in very handy in carrying my paint boxes and other paraphernalia on the trail." She spent time at Independence Monument documenting Otto's climb on canvas. (Courtesy of the *Grand Junction Daily News*.)

Horseback riders (bottom center) ride to Independence Monument on the opposite side from where the Otto-Farnham wedding ceremony was held. Otto's rock ladder was located along the right edge of the 500-foot monolith. The top rock platform is said to be approximately 6 feet wide. (Courtesy of the National Archives and Records Center, Denver.)

Beatrice Farnham had a dream to establish a girls' colony in Monument Canyon for poor city girls whose health would be enhanced by the clean air and sunshine. There Beatrice proposed to use her own family wealth to provide programs to make the American woman "the independent creature she should be." (Courtesy of the *Grand Junction Daily News*.)

VOL. XIII, NO. 153. GRAND JUNCTI

Girls Colony in Monument Canon Soon

Beatrice Farnham Otto, bride of John Otto, is proving herself not only an artist and nature lover but philanthropist as well. Her latest scheme to be announced here, but one that she has been working upon for over a year is the organization of a colony of Massachusetts girls in Bonument canon. Her original plan was to form a colony of poor girls from her own state in New Mexico but since her marriage to Otto, she has shifted the location of the colony to Monument canon, where she will have personal supervision over the girls.

Her colony will be in the nature of a sanitarium for poor girls in ill health, who can not afford to come to Colorado for sunshine and fresh air.

Mrs. Otto, who signs her name "Beatrice Otto" so that her bankers will receive her checks, is very well to do. A few years ago she purchased one of the oldest estates in Massachusetts at South Meymuth which she presented to her parents.

Otto later denied the validity of the "girls' colony" story: "Some valley scribe faked it. Perhaps it had its origin with the hiving of a swarm of bees which flew away from the valley, which we successfully accomplished before we left the canon last July. A colony of bees is a more reasonable proposition." (Photograph by Whipple Chester; courtesy of the Chester family.)

Two months after the wedding (and a three-week honeymoon), Beatrice Farnham headed back East, never to return to John again. She asked him to file the divorce papers and provided John with $2,000 in alimony. She got as far as Kansas, where she met up with cowboy Dallas Benson and they appeared together in a trick-riding exhibition. Their signature feat ironically was called "chasing the bride," where the pair galloped side-by-side; Beatrice then leapt from her saddle into the arms of her new husband amid the applause from the other cowboys. (Above, photograph by Whipple Chester; courtesy of the National Park Service; left, courtesy of the *Denver Post*.)

Three

THE GREAT GRAND MESA

When the summer heat made trail building difficult, John Otto worked elsewhere to fulfill his vision of uniting Mesa County's other natural resources into one national park. On the northern portion of the Grand Valley, the Little Bookcliffs mountain range creates the image of a shelf of books. East of the valley, the largest flat-topped mountain, Grand Mesa, stands sentinel over the fruit orchards.

On September 21, 1910, Otto began building the Sunbeam Trail to connect Mounts Garfield and Lincoln in the Little Bookcliffs across the palisades to the Grand Mesa. Schoolchildren bought "stock" in the trail project by pledging two bits for a paper stock certificate for Otto's autograph.

As the local paper reported, "Mr. Otto has undertaken the work without any hope of receiving adequate compensation for his services. He likes that sort of work and will be satisfied to secure sufficient funds to pay his living expenses and buy the powder and tools needed. It is the purpose to get all the children interested in securing at least that much for Mr. Otto and then they will be individually interested in the trail.

"It might be mentioned that not only is Mr. Otto performing an unselfish labor, for which we will long remember and thank him, but it would be difficult to find a better constructed path in the mountain regions. It would be almost impossible to find another man who would undertake such a task under the circumstances that he is doing this work. We should none of us withhold the little help and encouragement we can offer, as we would indeed be ungrateful not to recognize the work he is trying to do. . . . Mr. Otto is not asking pay for the time he puts in on this very commendable work, but he must have some funds to pay his living expenses and the people are being depended upon to give him assistance even in a small way."

John Otto continued the same trail-building finesse he demonstrated on the Colorado National Monument's Corkscrew Trail; this time, his summer trail-building project was on the Grand Mesa, across the valley from the monument. Switchbacks across a boulder field enabled horses, burros, and people to scale the nearly vertical cliffs. (Courtesy of the Benge family.)

Across a boulder field (called the Slash) that can be seen from Grand Junction, Otto (center) was able to build the Butterfly Trail, which brought people from the Little Bookcliff mountain range, across the palisades below the Grand Mesa, to the Sunbeam Trail that connected to the town of Clifton. (Courtesy of the Otto family.)

Otto began building the Sunbeam Trail in September 1910 with support from local businessmen. Palisade mayor John D. Reeder presented him with a new ceremonial pick. Otto expected to reach the palisades at the foot of Grand Mesa by Thanksgiving, when he planned to cease trail building and return to his work in the Colorado National Monument. "I want to continue the work in the Monument canon this winter," wrote Otto, "and start work on Grand Mesa next spring. In the meantime, I hope that the proposed wagon road to the top of Grand Mesa is a go." (Both, courtesy of the Otto family.)

Lining up for the trail.

Unlike the trails in the Colorado National Monument, Otto's Grand Mesa trails were more susceptible to storm damage and rock slides. He often returned to his trail work only to find he had to repeat the previous day's labor. Nevertheless, publicity he received on his work created continuous interest. On one Sunday, more than 100 people were counted on or near the trail, curious to see the work firsthand. The local newspaper reported, "Mr. Otto has undertaken the work without any hope of receiving adequate compensation for his services. He likes that sort of work and will be satisfied to secure sufficient funds to pay his living expenses and buy the powder and tools needed." (Both, courtesy of the Otto family.)

Top of Grand Mesa 10560 ft.

Otto wanted to unite the Colorado National Monument and the Grand Mesa into one large national park: "Let us have the Colorado national park. . . . in time it will become the great outdoor convention place; there's parking space for a million automobiles and room for the airplanes by the thousands, on top of the greatest and grandest of all mesas in Mesa county, Colorado. Join the Colorado National Park movement and you shall live forever! The first step is to get the right organization together, with headquarters in Grand Junction and with locals in all the towns in western Colorado. Before this month is over, we will have it on the way." (Both, courtesy of the Otto family.)

To carry his valley-wide national park proposal, Otto turned to the *Daily Sentinel* newspaper to champion his cause during World War I. He saw every spruce tree at the Colorado National Monument as a potential holder of a red, white, and blue banner. He saw the evergreen trees of the Grand Mesa as symbols of "ever living." Combined, his joint proposal represented the red, white, and blue colors living forever. In a letter to the director of the National Park Service, Otto proposed the "down deep" of the Colorado National Monument and the "high up" of the Grand Mesa could be combined as the Colorado National Park. (Both, courtesy of the Otto family.)

A committee of Grand Junction businessmen accepted Otto's invitation to see his trail-building progress on Grand Mesa. Fred Mantey, Paul Merise, Ole Nelson, Bill Wood (secretary of the chamber of commerce), Steve Hathaway (Independent Lumber Company), Bert Benge (shoe store owner), and Grant Wright (photojournalist for the *Daily News*) met Otto (above, pointing) at the trailhead. Otto prepared four burros and two horses to transfer the camping gear and supplies up the Wild Rose Trail. Along the way, posts with WRT painted on them identified the correct trail. Trees were notched with Otto's signatory four cuts, representing the red, white, and blue and the green of the pinion pine trees. (Both, courtesy of the Benge family.)

The harsh winter weather ended Otto's Grand Mesa trail-and-road system. The $3,000-per-mile cost and deep snow that wiped out the hairpin turns in the design were responsible. A 1926 newspaper reported, "The present road has not been found as satisfactory as desired, and unless it is found to be the best possible route, no further improvements will be made on it and it will be abandoned with construction of the new road. It is steep and winding, with innumerable sharp, blind curves. It is on a north slope where the snowfall is heavy and gathers in great drifts. After rains it remains wet and muddy for a long time because the sun does not reach it." (Both, courtesy of the Benge family.)

Four

OTTO'S SHORT-LIVED WILDLIFE PRESERVE

Trail building was not Otto's only forte. After the livestock were removed from the canyons, he envisioned the natural boundaries as a logical wildlife sanctuary. Deer naturally grazed the canyons, but Otto gained support from the local Elks Club to add a small herd of elk to the preserve. Schoolchildren collected buffalo nickels to raise funds to add bison.

The elk and deer migrated out of the park, often taking Otto's fencing with them. Even the Civilian Conservation Corps fencing added in 1934 failed as a deterrent to the bison. Quickly, the small herd overgrazed the sparse desert-like canyon floor, and the animals began to show evidence of inbreeding. When the Grand Junction Chamber of Commerce took it upon itself to harvest several elk and bison for a barbecue from "Otto's" private stock, they experienced Otto's letter-writing wrath.

Upon the natural death of "Johannes," the patriarch bull of the herd in 1945, custodian George T. Hopper wrote an obituary: "Having lived a full life of approximately one score and five, and fathered many progeny, as nearly as can be determined, he passed away quietly simultaneously with the announcement of the surrender of Japan at 5:00 o'clock on August 14th.

"As there was no evidence of empty bottles adjacent to the body, it is thought that death was not due to over celebration of this momentous event, but due to heart failure caused by shock at the announcement of the cessation of hostilities. . . . Having lived a secluded and solitary life for the past several years, since his one time power was usurped by one of his more virile progeny, none of his numerous family attended the services, nor were any of the bereaved widows observed. It was with mixed feelings that this callousness on the part of the immediate family was viewed."

In 1956, the herd was culled to 15 bison from 25 in 1956. Navaho Indians from several southwestern hogans dressed the carcasses. The remainder of the herd was removed in the 1970s when wildlife biologists and range managers found the canyon floor could no longer sustain the herd.

"I am planning on raising some more money by subscriptions from people in the valley to fence the park," John Otto wrote to the chief of field division in 1913. "It is part of the original plan to have a game refuge. There are some deer to start with. I have written to the Supervisor of the Wichita National Forest for four of the young buffalo out of the Gov. herd of between 40 and 50. We are trying to get a few elk from Wyoming. Of course it takes time to improve this Park for the benefit of the people of the whole state—anything done to help matters along under your direction will be greatly appreciated by many many people of our section here." (Courtesy of the author's collection.)

The newspapers said Otto was "agitating the matter for some time" among prominent businessmen, the American Bison Society, and other government agencies to add wildlife to the park. When a correspondent from *Collier's* planned to visit, Otto thought the writer would enjoy the scenic beauty of the canyons but would also appreciate "a little surprise for him and stage something that he would remember, and that would cause him to write about Grand Junction as the brightest, the best, the freshest little city in all the great wide west." (Above, courtesy of the National Park Service; right, courtesy of the Museum of Western Colorado.)

John Otto became such a familiar face to his herd of bison that he was able to approach the younger members of the herd. In the spring of 1926, the first calf was born at the Colorado National Monument. Additional bison were brought from Denver mountain parks. (Courtesy of the National Park Service.)

Bison were able to graze close to the fence outside the canyons of the Colorado National Monument. Occasionally, orchard owners found the animals to be unwanted visitors among their fruit trees, thanks to fencing that failed to hold up to a bison bull who found it to be a convenient scratching post. (Courtesy of the National Archives and Records Administration, Denver.)

Point Wilson Fence, as it became known, enclosed the east gap in the south wall of Monument Canyon in 1923. Long cedar posts packed in by burros from a bench a mile or so away were dropped over the rim, tethered to 400-foot wire cables. Three feet of heavy netting and six additional feet of wire above the mesh made a formidable barrier to retain deer, elk, and other animals. The fence was approximately the length of two city blocks, erected across gulches and around large boulders. When this author visited the fence in 1976, there was little damage to the fence Otto created for his wildlife park more than 50 years earlier. (Right, courtesy of the National Park Service; below, courtesy of the author's collection.)

More than a decade after Otto single-handedly built his Point Wilson Fence in the Colorado National Monument, the government-sponsored Civilian Conservation Corps (CCC) strengthened the wildlife boundary in the 1930s with their own fencing project. Iron posts replaced the pinion wood Otto salvaged among the trees in the Monument. Men employed by the corps prepared to set posts that were dragged to the spot by teams of mules because the terrain was too rough for access by a truck. The CCC and other relief organizations continued Otto's legacy of trail and road building after he left the park in the early 1930s. (Both, courtesy of the National Archives and Records Administration, Denver.)

Five

CCC CAMPS AND OTTO'S HIGHWAY DREAM

Other than foot-and-hoof trails along the canyon floor, the canyon walls of the Colorado National Monument were nearly insurmountable to the average visitor. The Trail of the Serpent, a 2.5-mile trail with 54 switchbacks, was later expanded to a wagon road from a footpath but still had the stigma of being called "the most dangerous road ever built." The trail passed through the eastern slope of the Monument and ended at a rock promontory whose impressive cliff edge was known as Cold Shivers Point.

John Otto and the Grand Junction Chamber of Commerce sought to improve access into the canyons of the Colorado National Monument. They proposed a 24-mile, single-width highway to the Fruita end of the park along the same route that is now the Scenic Rim Drive. The unlikely duo, through subscription and gifts from local residents, raised $1,500.

U.S. president Franklin Delano Roosevelt's Civil Works Administration accepted the $1,500 as seed money for publicly subscribed funds to include the road proposal as a federal project. In November 1931, chief engineer Frank A. Kittredge of the National Park Service and road engineer T. W. Secrest submitted plans for the double-width rim rock road. For reasons unknown, John Otto left the monument at this time, and Clifford Anderson from Yellowstone National Park was installed as custodian of the Colorado National Monument.

In May 1933, the Civilian Conservation Corps (CCC) camp at the east entrance and a second camp at the Fruita entrance flanked the road project. The Works Project Administration added a transient camp on the eastern end of the project, putting rail-riding hobos to work installing 5.2 miles of a water main and other roadway improvements.

Roadwork continued until 1942, when World War II called custodians and rangers to active duty. Work on the road resumed in the fall of 1949. The final project is 23 miles long, connecting the two entrances that are actually only 8 miles apart. The landfill necessary to traverse the sheer walls and the construction of three tunnels assisted in earning recognition by the National Register of Historic Places in 1993.

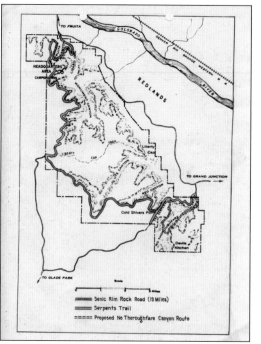

Before John Otto left the Colorado National Monument, he envisioned extending the 54 switchbacks of the Trail of the Serpent at the east entrance, blazing a rim-rock drive across the top of the canyon walls, and returning visitors to the western entrance near the town of Fruita. The roadway replaced portions of his foot-and-hoof trails with a road system that accommodated the advent of the transcontinental automobile "fad." His Union Trail would connect all the national parks with similar roads so travelers had scenic destinations to visit while traveling across the country. (Both, courtesy of the National Archives and Records Administration, Denver.)

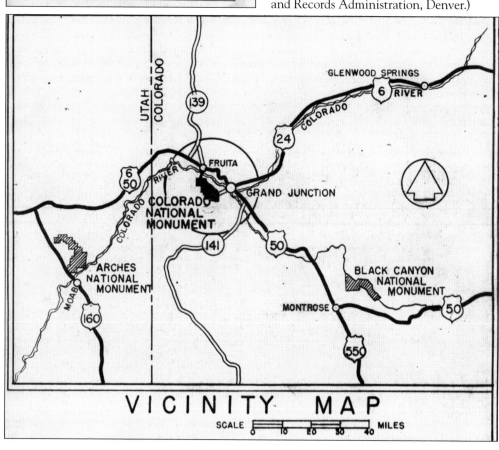

After the Civilian Conservation Corps contract was established in 1931, proposed monument improvements included roads, trails, a custodian's residence, and water main and campground development projects. Six local and federal relief organizations provided the funding through the Grand Junction Chamber of Commerce, Civilian Works Administration, and National Park Service emergency agencies. (Courtesy of the Colorado Historical Society.)

Construction crew workers from the Civilian Conservation Corps team in the Colorado National Monument pause at the truck shed for a picture in 1939. The Federal Unemployment Relief Act of 1933 was U.S. president Franklin Delano Roosevelt's proposal to alleviate unemployment during the Great Depression. (Courtesy of the Colorado State Archives.)

Tunnel
Scenic Rim Road in

Frank A. Kittredge, chief engineer for the National Park Service, and Thomas W. Secrest, park service engineer, viewed the grade necessary to build an automobile road from the valley floor of No Thoroughfare Canyon near Grand Junction to the rim rocks above the Monument canyons and return to the valley floor near Fruita Canyon on the western side of the park. Fill

Tunnel

...icinity of the tunnels

dirt between the canyon walls and three tunnels would be carved through the rock walls. Several "half tunnels" were also proposed. Some fill dirt for the roadbed was already deposited below the second marked tunnel and in the right panel of the panorama. (Courtesy of the National Archives Records Administration, Denver.)

Tunnel construction began with a "pilot hole" made in the rock walls to establish rock construction and disclose any unseen faults or hidden springs. Excavated rock dug from the pilot holes became the foundation for the approaches to the tunnel. Compressed-air jackhammers were used to bore away at the sandstone cliff wall. Half the steel drill-bits were sharpened in town while the other half were being used on the cliffs above town. Grand Junction's mild winter weather enabled construction to continue throughout the year. (Above, courtesy of the National Archives and Records Administration, Denver; below, courtesy of the National Park Service.)

The lower portal of Pilot Tunnel No. 1 shows excavated rock high enough to nearly obliterate the entrance to the tunnel. Workers use mining-style handcarts to transport the rock to the edge of the fill dirt between the canyon walls. (Courtesy of the National Archives and Records Administration, Denver.)

Once the tunnels were clear, the excavated tunnel rock blended with the fill dirt that served as the road base for the Scenic Rim Rock Drive through the Colorado National Monument. Original plans to build formal frames around the entrances of the tunnels were scrapped to provide a natural appearance. (Photograph by Wegeman; courtesy of the National Park Service.)

Station 462 of the Rim Rock Drive required the Civilian Conservation Corps engineers to bridge the canyon walls with fill dirt. Near the upper portal of Tunnel No. 2 (above), extensive fill was required. Other sections of the road relied on existing bedrock and only needed fill dirt from the tunnels to level the roadbed. The photograph below is at the upper portal of Tunnel No. 1. Fill dirt was often dropped from the rim rocks above the roadway and leveled predominately by hand by teams of laborers and mules. (Both, courtesy of the National Archives and Records Administration, Denver.)

Landscape architects, overseeing the construction of the Rim Rock Drive through the Colorado National Monument, were critical of construction scarring on the rock walls above the roadway. CCC workers were required to smooth down the aftermath of the dynamite drill holes on the rock walls. (Courtesy of the National Archives and Records Administration, Denver.)

Construction of the Fruita Tunnels on the west end of the monument required dynamiting rock walls in addition to filling dirt to support the roadbed between the tunnels. A small wooden building on the roadbed provided an emergency shelter to protect workers in case of falling loose rocks. (Courtesy of the National Park Service.)

The lower entrance of Upper Tunnel No. 1 was reported to contain "massive and unjointed" rock that was interlinked to hold together without lining. As a precaution, gunite was sprayed to create an additional skin on the tunnel walls to minimize any loose rocks or dirt from dropping onto the roadway. The work was done by National Park Service day laborers in 1937. Gunite is a mixture of Portland cement, fine aggregate, and water sprayed onto a wire mesh with a pneumatic device on existing rock-cut slopes. It is tinted to match the surrounding natural rock. (Photographs by Fred C. Hill; courtesy of the National Park Service.)

The roof at the center of the upper tunnel (above) showed the layers of rock. Fragment cracks were scaled off, leaving the roof of the tunnel in self-supporting condition. Wire mesh (below) was attached to the rock walls before spraying gunite to the mesh. The fresh gunite was covered with burlap and kept wet for five days while the application cured. The experimental process continued to be used in federal aid projects in Denver and Mesa Verde National Park. A moving platform was mounted to mining-style tracks and provided an emergency shelter for those working in fresh-cut tunnels. (Both, courtesy of the National Archives and Records Administration, Denver.)

A July 1933 blast along the Rim Rock Drive provided the Civilian Conservation Corps an opportunity to adopt John Otto's original vision overlooking the canyons. That year, the amount of rock-drilling dust prompted the CCC camp doctor to pull his men out of the "half-tunnel" excavation project. They were replaced by local hires from another government rock project. Unfortunately, on their first day of work, a rock outcrop dropped on the men, trapping some under the rock and hurling others over the adjacent 300-foot cliff. Most of the eight victims were young married men, some with young children. (Courtesy of the National Park Service.)

When CCC laborer Leroy Lewis was asked who should get credit for the work on the Colorado National Monument's "Road Around the Rimrock," he replied, "My opinion is that there was enough rock moved, holes drilled, dynamite and black powder expended in the years the road was under construction that all can take credit for it. The building of the Rim Rock Drive was the combined effort of many workers, all of whom can take satisfaction in their accomplishment." The photograph below shows enrollees working on the rock cut on the new Trail of the Serpent portion of the Colorado National Monument Scenic Rim Rock Drive. (Above, courtesy of the National Park Service; below, courtesy of the Colorado State Archives.)

Guard walls like these were built of natural stone harvested from the various rock cuts made to excavate the Scenic Rim Rock Road. Landscape architects assigned to the Civilian Conservation Corps construction sought to make all new construction blend into the natural beauty of the Colorado National Monument. Despite security details at either end of the road, local motorists were losing patience driving across the graded roadway. Signs were posted to use the road at their own risk while government laborers continued to build safety barriers and other refinements for the comfort of the motoring public. (Both, courtesy of the National Archives and Records Administration, Denver.)

The 1936 masonry wall near the Saddlehorn campground adjacent to the Visitors' Center was also built of rubble gathered during dynamite blasting for the roadway. Stonemason Dominic D'Angelo (pictured below) used his professional carving expertise to fit the stone with precision. Most travelers only see the topmost portions of the retaining walls that provide reinforcement of the roadway and reduce the potential for erosion during severe summer storms. Several Italian stone carvers were specifically recruited for their particular expertise. (Both, courtesy of the National Archives and Records Administration, Denver.)

The road in No Thoroughfare Canyon to replace the Trail of the Serpent was nearing completion in 1950 when the *Daily Sentinel* was invited on a press tour. Instead of traveling along 54 switchbacks in 2.5 miles and a grade of approximately 13 percent, the new road has an 8-percent grade with only a few switchbacks. (Courtesy of the National Park Service.)

Completion of the road near Cold Shivers Point required reducing the slopes of dirt excavated by dynamite blasting and excavating rock shoulders along the road. Care was given to reduce any impact to the surrounding foliage in order to maintain as much of the natural vegetation as possible. (Courtesy of the National Archives and Records Administration, Denver.)

Between 1933 and 1934, more than $250,000 was spent to complete approximately half of the rough grading that was needed in the first section of the Colorado National Monument. Laborers manually loaded the handcarts with the dynamited rubble, and mules pulled the carts along mine-like rail tracks to where the fill was needed to establish a roadbed for the Scenic Rim Rock Drive. The handcarts could be tilted to dump the rock to widen the roadway between canyons and ravines. Many of the workers for this labor were recruited among transients riding the railroad line that passed through Grand Junction and Fruita. (Both, courtesy of the National Park Service.)

World War II drew "the cream of the able-bodied men" from the CCC projects for recruitment into the military. Every few days, notices appeared in the local newspapers seeking 3,000 men to complete the roadwork before winter weather arrived. During World War II, National Park Service administrators discussed using the camps as Japanese internment camps or using German war prisoners for work in the Colorado National Monument. Because of the fear of sabotage and negative public opinion, the concept was short-lived and was never implemented. (Above, courtesy of the Colorado State Archives; below, courtesy of the National Archives and Records Administration, Denver.)

The Civilian Conservation Corps built 17 barracks at the Colorado National Monument to house hundreds of men during the construction projects. At the conclusion of the primary phase prior to World War II, the War Department and the National Park Service kept several buildings. Twenty-nine CCC buildings were presented to the Grand Junction Goodwill Industries through the efforts of L. W. Wilson, president of the Goodwill board of directors. Several of the remaining buildings kept in place at the Colorado National Monument were proposed to be used for Boy and Girl Scouts overnight camps and for church organizations. Buildings located south of Fruita were presented to the Redlands community by the U.S. Department of Agriculture. (Both, courtesy of the National Park Service.)

The National Park Service remodeled this one-story frame building, which had been originally constructed by the army CCC for use as officers' quarters in 1934, in 1946 for living quarters. The three-room building and shower bath contained a kitchen, living room, and one bedroom heated with a coal stove and had running water. (Courtesy of the National Archives and Records Administration, Denver.)

The maintenance area for the Colorado National Monument CCC camps were similar to the barracks used by the men. Equipment used in road construction was maintained close to the construction site. Most of the buildings were dismantled after the close of the project and were donated for civilian purposes to nonprofit organizations. (Courtesy of the National Park Service.)

The army CCC infirmary was built in 1934, and even after being remodeled by the National Park Service in 1941 for temporary living quarters, it was considered to be in poor condition five years later. The four rooms and shower bath included a kitchen, living room, and two bedrooms. (Courtesy of the National Archives and Records Administration, Denver.)

Fruita Camp NM-3-C (National Monument, Camp 3, Colorado) was built of canvas army tents on platforms. When much-improved wooden barracks replaced the tents, the men dubbed the new camp the "Taj Mahal." Accommodations included a peg to hang clothes, a coal stove for heat, and a line of cots with no privacy. (Courtesy of the National Park Service.)

The postwar road construction crews were responsible for completing the new Rim Rock Drive so the National Park Service could abandon John Otto's Trail of the Serpent. This would create a new eastern gravel road to the Monument. As W. M. Wood, secretary of the Grand Junction Chamber of Commerce, explained in a letter to Rep. Robert F. Rockwell, "Considering the tremendous amount of interest evidenced throughout the nation in the Monument, and in view of the fact that the present Trail of the Serpent is a really hazardous approach, particularly for strangers, it does not seem reasonable that an additional delay would be permitted." (Both, courtesy of the National Archives and Records Administration, Denver.)

Laborers in 1943 received salaries slightly below comparable wages. Common labor received 50¢ per hour plus just less than $1 overtime for eight hours. Light truck drivers received a dime more per hour. Boys 16 to 18 years of age had to provide proof of age, be suited to age and strength, avoid hazardous occupations and those detrimental to health or welfare, and work no more than eight hours a day for six consecutive days. Boys received the same wages paid to adults for similar work. (Above, courtesy of the National Park Service; below, courtesy of the Colorado State Archives.)

In order to reduce the danger of accidents on the Trail of the Serpent, all National Park Service, Civilian Conservation Corps, and Work Project Administration drivers had to follow these instructions: (1) When descending the Trail of the Serpent, all cars and trucks shall drive on the extreme right side of the road at a speed which will allow the driver to stop his car or truck

within the distance which he can see immediately ahead; (2) Before starting down, each driver shall reduce gears; (3) When meeting a car or truck that is coming up the trail, the descending car or truck shall come to a complete stop until the ascending car or truck has passed. (Courtesy of the author's collection.)

A Civilian Conservation Corps photograph looks up the grade on one of the numerous sharp curves of the Trail of the Serpent. The highway is supported on the outer edge of the ledge rock by embankments created from dynamited rock wedged into natural fallen boulders. The road had an overall width of 14 to 18 feet, and even in the 1940s, the road was considered to be in "a sad state of repair" by the civil engineers. After the road was closed to motor vehicles, the bottom 1976 view of the Trail of the Serpent as a footpath (left) shows it returning to a natural state. The reinforcement rock (center) provides some support to the trail. (Both, courtesy of the author's collection.)

Before the Grand Valley communities began "boosting" the benefits of the region and the majesty of the Colorado National Monument, Grand Mesa, and Little Bookcliffs, access to the monument from Grand Junction required an isolated drive across the old cattle grazing plains. The only access was the challenging Trail of the Serpent. (Courtesy of the National Archives and Records Administration, Denver.)

An opposing view from the valley looking back toward the Colorado National Monument shows the most logical design location for the Trail of the Serpent against the far escarpment. A previous road, the Gordon Toll Road, bypassed the Monument on a grade left of No Thorough Canyons. (Courtesy of the National Archives and Records Administration, Denver.)

A view of the "big cut" was photographed by CCC engineers in mid-December 1949. The rock blasted through the outcrop would be used to provide a base for the roadway between the canyons. Laborer Leroy Lewis described the construction sites as "lots of holes, some as deep as 16 feet, were drilled, and the dynamite was tamped into them and the sound of 'Fire in the hole!' caused everyone to take cover. 'Dog holes' were drilled into the sandstone, filled with lots of black powder, which caused a less violent explosion than dynamite. That meant we had lots of rock to move, but it did not disturb the landscape as much. The men were constantly reminded that this was a 'National Monument,' and it was to remain in the pristine natural state as far as possible." (Both, courtesy of the National Archives Records Administration, Denver.)

After road grading, laborers reset rock along the roadway from the tunnel and other dynamite-blasting projects. The bank sloping, in Section D, helped mitigate runoff erosion during sporadic but intense summer thunderstorms. (Courtesy of the National Archives and Records Administration, Denver.)

The area now occupied by the Colorado National Monument's Visitors' Center served as a parking lot for the Izaak Walton League picnic in 1951. The screen in the center of the picture served as a temporary backstop for a softball game. (Courtesy of the National Archives and Records Administration, Denver.)

Laborers are loading a mixture of rock and dirt from the rock quarry for toe slopes along the Rim Rock Drive. Much of the work was done by hand labor and small trucks, manually shoveling the rock. (Photograph by C. M. Shannon; courtesy of the Colorado State Archives.)

Progress is made in Sections 1036 and 1039 on the Rim Rock Drive. A shovel (center) is preparing a pilot road for construction traffic and for carting material for removing the rock from the lower switchback that was pushed over the slope. (Courtesy of the National Archives and Records Administration, Denver.)

In addition to the Civilian Conservation Corps projects within the Colorado National Monument, Work Project Administration road projects employed 200 men for three months to complete the sub-grade over the roadway and bring the bed to the proper grade. After installing a culvert through one of the draws across the roadway, laborers leveled the roadway over the culvert. Beside the quality of the food, one of the major complaints from laborers was the lack of work gloves to prevent hand blisters. (Both, courtesy of the National Park Service.)

CCC laborers intentionally obliterated the winding "Old Water Supply Road" (which originally was John Otto's trail for the Fruita entrance to the Colorado National Monument). The new access road (located above the old trail) is under construction to a point at the center of the picture. (Courtesy of the National Archives and Records Administration, Denver.)

With the gravel road completed along the Rim Rock Drive, motorists were finally able to drive along the approximate route originally envisioned by John Otto in the 1920s. The road was initially accessible by the old Trail of the Serpent until laborers were able to carve a new access route near the Grand Junction entrance. (Courtesy of the National Archives and Records Administration, Denver.)

Between 1938 and 1941, approximately $3,875,000 was spent for two Civilian Conservation Corps camps and other large government-relief crew, road and trail crews, and transient camps. They built 19 miles of Rim Rock Drive, the ranger residence, a picnic area, a shelter house at the east entrance, fence for the buffalo, a telephone line, a water line, and reservoirs. Little work was done during World War II until $138,700 was appropriated between 1949 and 1951. In the travel years of 1937–1938, a total of 64,915 visitors traveled through the monument in 15,385 vehicles, while construction continued on the Rim Rock Drive. (Both, courtesy of the National Archives and Records Administration, Denver.)

The Colorado National Monument includes hills and cliffs that parallel the Colorado River for approximately 10 miles. Two to four miles from the river, the red sandstone cliffs rise abruptly above the Grand Valley to an altitude approximately 2,500 feet above the river. It is nearly impossible to climb out of the box canyons of No Thoroughfare, Red, Ute, Monument, and Fruita. As an internal National Park Service memorandum in 1947 stated, "The canyons are not so great as to create a feeling of abhorrence or fear, but creates a desire to appreciate the views and a wish to get down among the formations." (Both, courtesy of National Archives Records Administration, Denver.)

National Park Service engineers evaluated the Rim Rock Drive following the completion of the road. The photograph above incorporates the natural contours of the Colorado National Monument with dynamited cuts into the rock outcropping above the road, fill to create a road base, and forage restoration to reinstall natural vegetation. The photograph below shows a typical view of one of the through-rock cuts on the drive across the mesa. The road was constructed to a 24-foot shoulder-to-shoulder grade width and provided with a sandstone spall-base plated with a fine sand or silt. (Both, courtesy of the National Archive and Records Administration, Denver.)

Ever since John Otto left his tent and other rustic accommodations behind, the National Park Service sought to provide civilized accommodations for future Colorado National Monument custodians. The CCC laborers built a one-story stone building with a half concrete basement equipped with a hot-air furnace, laundry trays, and a shingle roof in 1934. The floor plan included a kitchen with a breakfast nook, living room, and two bedrooms. The one-car garage (shown under construction below) was separate from the house. Grounds were partially landscaped to complement the forage in the Colorado National Monument. (Both, courtesy of the National Archives and Records Administration, Denver.)

Italian stonemasons who assembled the retaining wall rock work along the Rim Rock Drive, provided the craftsmanship to build the custodian's house and garage. Only the most pristine rock was quarried from the road construction projects along the Rim Rock Drive. The stone carvers squared the blocks and hand-assembled the house and garage walls with precision. A Civilian Conservation Corps enrollee named Moberly was enlisted as supervisor for much of the precision stonework because of his expertise as a civilian stonecutter. Stonemason Dominic D'Angelo also provided his civilian services. (Both, courtesy of the National Archives and Records Administration, Denver.)

A National Park Service memorandum in 1937 read, "To adequate protect the large Federal investment, the whole monument highway must be gravel surfaced and oiled, preferably by contract under Bureau of Public Roads supervision. . . . Local communities, travel agencies and potential visitors from all over the United States, are bringing increasing pressure to bear on this office and the Washington office of the National Park Service to hasten the day of finally completing this spectacular highway through an important scenic area for public enjoyment. The public has watched construction progress for six years now, and is growing increasingly impatient for final completion of the through Colorado National Monument highway." The memo was written by Superintendent Jesse L. Nusbaum. (Courtesy of the National Archive and Records Administration, Denver.)

Six

DINOSAURS ALMOST ENTER THE MONUMENT

A Mesa County dentist and member of the Western Colorado Academy of Sciences, Dr. S. M. Bradbury, contacted Dr. Elmer S. Riggs of Chicago's Field Museum in 1899 to explain that local residents have collected dinosaur bones since 1885. Dr. Riggs visited the site in 1900 and discovered portions of a camarasaurus and brachiosaurus dinosaur skeleton near what would become the west entrance of the Colorado National Monument. The following year, Riggs unearthed two-thirds of an apatosaurus in the same area. The evidence was brought to the Field Museum, where they reportedly created a sensation among museum visitors.

In 1929, a *Daily Sentinel* advertising man and local historian and others found additional evidence of plant and animal life that roamed the county during the time of the dinosaurs. Likewise, Edwin Holt, a teacher at the Grand Junction Junior College (now Mesa State College), found another dinosaur skeleton a few hundred feet away from the Riggs discovery.

Civilian Conservation Corps laborers excavated the site and found additional reptilian skeletons including allosaurus, stegosaurus, and diplodocus. Two others—mososaurus and brontosaurus—were found near the Trail of the Serpent near the Grand Junction entrance of the Monument.

The local discoveries prompted Bryan Patterson of the Field Museum to study the area between 1932 and 1947 for additional dinosaur-era deposits. Al Look, Dr. Riggs, and the Grand Junction Chamber of Commerce underwrote a bronze plaque, recognizing the discoveries of Riggs and others.

In 1938, it was proposed that Riggs Hill and its fossils be included as part of Colorado National Monument. However, souvenir hunters stripped the site of many of the remaining dinosaur bones. After additional vandalism occurred, the Bureau of Land Management reburied the site in 1983. The 200-foot hill was located in portions of seven different 40-acre tracts of Bureau of Land Management land.

Today the site is open during daylight hours to the public along a self-guided trail. Many of the bones excavated by the academic archeological expeditions are now on display at the Museum of Western Colorado.

A 1938 photograph looking east at Riggs Hill identifies the location of the dinosaur quarry (letter A). Most of the rocks belong to the Morrison formation, alternating with beds of sandstone. The high point of the hill is capped with a ledge of hard black or brown sandstone that broke off and rolled down the slopes. (Photograph by Edwin Holt; courtesy of the National Archives and Records Administration, Denver.)

An archeologist posed next to 25 vertebrae from a skeleton of a brachiosaurus's tail (approximately 15 feet long) on Riggs Hill adjacent to the Colorado National Monument. The tibia, or lower leg, of the largest land animal is in the upper right corner of the picture. The lower leg is 6.5 feet long. (Courtesy of the National Archives and Records Administration, Denver.)

Left of the hammer (lower center) are the long tail spikes and some ribs of a stegosaurus on Riggs Hill. The tip of the tail vertebrae (above the spikes) is approximately one inch in diameter. They increase in size to approximately 4 inches near Edwin Holt's pick near the top center of the photograph. (Courtesy of the National Archives and Records Administration, Denver.)

The allosaurus was a carnivorous dinosaur. Approximately 20 vertebrae of the tail are located right of the whisk broom (center). Two forelegs are right and above the broom. The shoulder blade is located at the top center of the photograph; several ribs and a 7-inch claw were also found at the Riggs Hill site. (Courtesy of the National Archives and Records Administration, Denver.)

Arno B. Cammerer, director of the National Park Service (1933–1940), visited the Riggs Hill site for possible inclusion into the Colorado National Monument. The nearest point of the monument is approximately a half-mile from the Holt Dinosaur Quarry on the west slope of Riggs Hill. (Courtesy of the National Park Service.)

The 29 vertebrae of a stegosaurus tail measured approximately 13 feet. At the end of the tail, four vertical spikes were approximately 2 feet long (left of the whisk broom several feet in front of Edwin Holt). Two dermal plates (2 feet long and triangular in shape) are located next to the tail vertebrae. (Courtesy of the National Park Service.)

Seven

COLORADO NATIONAL MONUMENT

During the first 50 years of the Colorado National Monument, a series of custodians were responsible for maintaining one of the state's scenic locations. Between 1911 and the mid-1960s, John Otto, Arthur T. Gormley, Clifford L. Anderson, Breynton R. Finch, John F. Aiton, George T. Hopper, Russell L. Mahan, Homer W. Robinson, Fred Bussey, and Robert Benton were among the first custodians and superintendents dedicated to the preservation of the canyons, red rocks, and monoliths of the Colorado National Monument.

Prior to the opening of the park to modern visitors, the first people associated with the area were known as the Basket Maker II and III people, who farmed the valley sometime after 300 AD. Two mummies found near the monument have been documented. After the Basket Makers, artifacts attributed to the Pueblos indicate their presence between 700 AD and 1600 AD. Their heritage was continued by the Ute Indians, who called the Grand Valley home until they were moved out in September 1881.

Spanish expeditions in 1776 led by Padres Escalante and Dominguez are documented in the valley. Likewise, trappers frequented the Western Slope between 1815 and 1845. The only fur-trading post was established by Joseph Roubdeau in approximately 1839 near the present site of Grand Junction.

On September 7, 1881, O. D. Russell and William McGinley staked the first ranch near Roubdeau's trading post. George A. Crawford followed that homestead the same month. Crawford formed the Grand Junction Town Company on October 10, 1881. The following year, the Denver and Rio Grande Railroad reached the site. William E. Pabor platted the town of Fruita in 1884.

With the opening of the Colorado National Monument and Rim Rock Drive, thousands of tourists visit the once-inaccessible canyons of the monument under the guidance of the U.S. National Park Service.

John Otto would have been proud.

Among the $12-a-year men who served as the Colorado National Monument's first custodians was John Otto. As reported by the U.S. Department of the Interior, "The records in the case of the Colorado National Monument . . . show that Mr. Otto has been a very patriotic and public-spirited citizen in that at his own expense he has built many trails in the region now covered by the National Monument for the purpose of enabling visitors to see, with some degree of safety in travel, the principal and most extraordinary of the natural features existing there. He has been recommended as eminently fitted for the duties of custodian and I believe that he will accept the appointment under the conditions named. Such appointment will not only be very acceptable to the people of Colorado, but he will be faithful to the trust with which he is charged." (Courtesy of the Chester family.)

Art Gormley was a likely replacement for John Otto when he "resigned" from the position of custodian of the Monument. Gormley accepted the position on May 1, 1927, but he quickly became overwhelmed by conflicts between Otto's wildlife fencing plans and those of the Grand Junction Chamber of Commerce. Approximately five months after accepting the position, he resigned the post, which was taken over by the Grand Junction Chamber of Commerce. (Courtesy of the Gormley family.)

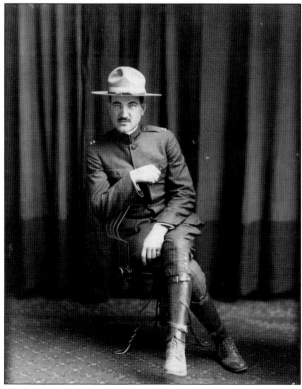

Frank Merriell, mayor of Fruita, was one of Otto's two nemeses who did not appreciate Otto's eccentric ideas for the Colorado National Monument. Quietly he tried to work behind Otto's back to replace the first superintendent of the Monument by writing venomous letters to the National Park Service officials in Washington, D.C. (Courtesy of the author's collection.)

Stephen T. Mather came to Washington, D.C., as special assistant to Secretary of the Interior Franklin K. Lane for national park concerns. Through his insistence, Congress successfully created the National Park Service in 1916 and appointed Mather as the first director (1917–1928). (Courtesy of the National Park Service.)

Horace Albert joined the Department of the Interior at the age of 23, assisting Mather's National Park Service initiative. He was appointed assistant director in 1917 and served as superintendent of Yellowstone National Park from 1919 to 1929 before being appointed as National Park Service director from 1929 to 1933. (Courtesy of the National Park Service.)

Arno B. Cammerer replaced Albright as assistant director of the National Park Service in 1919 before becoming associate director in 1928 and director (1933–1940). During his period in office, the National Park Service became active in recreational area planning and management, and supervised the Civilian Conservation Corps. (Courtesy of the National Park Service.)

Arthur E. Demaray left the U.S. Geological Survey when the National Park Service was staffed in 1917. His brief tenure as National Park Service director in 1951 before his retirement included work to incorporate the National Park Service with the New Deal in the wartime years. (Courtesy of the National Park Service.)

In 1949, Hollywood discovered the Colorado National Monument. Robert Taylor, James Stewart, and Debra Paget starred in the controversial Western *Devil's Doorway*, the first film to portray Native Americans as something other than bloodthirsty savages or primitives. Filming was predominately done in No Thoroughfare Canyon on the eastern portion of the monument. (Courtesy of the National Park Service.)

After the MGM cast received instructions prior to filming a battle scene between Native Americans and sheep men, director Anthony Mann executed the confrontation before the cameras. Lighting personnel, wranglers, and other production crewmembers stand by at the bottom of the picture. No casualties were reported. (Courtesy of the National Park Service.)

The production lasted approximately two weeks in the No Thoroughfare Canyon area of the national monument. *Devil's Doorway* was released the same year as a better-known film on the same subject, *Broken Arrow*. Because the Anthony Mann production was more realistic, the film was held back for a quiet release without much public or critical attention. (Courtesy of the National Park Service.)

Hollywood actors portraying sheep ranchers trail a flock in a scene shot outside of the Colorado National Monument on the north side of the Grand Junction entrance. Other Hollywood films have briefly included the Colorado National Monument, but John Badham's 1985 production of *American Flyers* made the monument a featured component of his film about a bicycle race. (Courtesy of National Archives Records Administration, Denver.)

Several Grand Junction residents took up John Otto's propensity to become local "boosters" of the Colorado National Monument. From left to right are W. M. Wood, manager of the Grand Junction Chamber of Commerce; Charles Rump, an enthusiastic backer of the Colorado National Monument; Robert Grant, a *Daily Sentinel* news photographer; and Frank H. Reeds, a *Daily Sentinel* reporter. (Courtesy of the National Archives and Records Administration, Denver.)

Park rangers responsible for the Colorado National Monument in 1956 include, from left to right, Monte Fitch (chief ranger), Alvie Redden (seasonal ranger), Hap Foster (seasonal ranger), Ray Spruill (seasonal ranger), Mural Messersmith, and John Aragon. Homer W. Robinson (not pictured) served as superintendent under the joint administration of the Colorado and Black Canyon of the Gunnison National Monuments. (Courtesy of the National Park Service.)

The Grand Valley of Western Colorado is internationally known for the fruit trees that grow in a climate created by the Little Bookcliff mountains and the Grand Mesa. Likewise, the Colorado National Monument rapidly gained international interest from journalists who admired the efforts to make these sites accessible to the public. Cross-marketing developed as Colorado fruit growers began to capitalize on the marketing of the Colorado National Monument adjacent to the peach orchards on the Redlands outside the monument. The "Garden of the Rockies" reflected the orchards as well as the canyon lands of the Colorado National Monument. (Above, courtesy of Steve and Denise Hight; right, courtesy of the National Archives and Records Administration, Denver.)

Above is the Coke Ovens and Independence Monument; below is Balanced Rock. The *Daily Sentinel* in 1938 reported on the scenic benefits of the Colorado National Monument: "Fame of the Colorado National Monument was spread across the country by thousands of tourists who included the area in their itinerary last summer. Registration books at the monument's entrances showed the best tourist season on record, and cars from every state in the Union and Canada were noted. Rising 1,000 to 2,000 feet above the Grand Valley and seamed with many highly colored canons, the monument contains magnificent examples of massive erosion, including lofty monoliths that stand out from sheer canyon walls like giant sentinels." (Both, courtesy of the National Park Service.)

Rock climbers rest on the top of Independence Monument. The following description comes from an internal National Park Service report about the area: "The brilliant red sandstone of the Entrada formation, capped by the gray-white of the Morrison, both of Jurassic age, have been carved by nature in beautiful and picturesque forms. The most prominent of the sandstone monoliths is Independence rock, 500 feet high, 250 feet long, and 100 feet wide at the base. Surrounding it are many others of nearly equal height. Jefferson Monument is more than 400 feet high, almost round, with a diameter of 100 feet at its base. Fisherman's head [Kissing Couple], nearly 400 feet high, is surmounted by a colossal, yet vivid presentation of a human countenance with cap tilted down to the eyes. While the monoliths are primarily features of the monument, there are also numerous caves and passageways." (Courtesy of the National Park Service.)

Above is the Monument Valley; below are the Coke Ovens. An internal National Park Service report described the areas: "In great cliff walls and natural amphitheatres, petrified wood, dinosaur remains, and evidences of early habitations of American aborigines are found. Deer, elk, and buffalo range in the area, which, like all the national parks and monuments, is a game sanctuary in which no hunting is permitted. A wide, spectacular scenic rim highway is being constructed by the national park service. This highway traverses the most attractive and spectacular sections of this monument, and connects with Transcontinental Highway No. 50—both at Fruita and Grand Junction." (Both, courtesy of the National Park Service.)

Above is Monument Canyon; below is Liberty Cap. The National Park Service described the area as follows: "This partially completed scenic drive is now open to tourist travel. From it visitors obtain splendid views of the Devil's Kitchen, Cold Shivers Point, Miracle Rock, the Coke Ovens, and other attractive formations. From the summit, a magnificent panorama may be had. To the north, the majestic range of the Book Cliff mountains, towers in the sky; to the east, the most famous of all flat-top mountains, the Grand Mesa, stretches as far as the eye can see; nearer at hand, the Colorado river rewinds through the verdant Grand valley with its countless orchards." (Both, courtesy of the National Park Service.)

Shown above is Kissing Couple or Fisherman's Rock; below is Monument Canyon. Throughout the years, many people wrote about the Colorado National Monument. With rock formations created long before mankind populated the area, the observations of the canyons remain as fresh today as they were when John Otto first began boosting the beauty of this portion of Western Colorado. With the completion of the Scenic Rim Rock Drive, the National Park Service was free to invite photographers and scribes to bring the pictures and word descriptions of their visit to the rest of the world. (Both, courtesy of the National Park Service.)

Above is Independence Monument; below is a view of Devil's Kitchen. The *Daily News* challenged the Grand Junction Chamber of Commerce to provide the people with a cool and attractive resort and park close to the city: "Grand Junction is hot in the summer time. We need that heat in the manufacture of our peaches and red apples, but towards the weekend we also very humanly long for a lungful of the keen air of the upper reaches. And this is just what Monument Park offers us. . . . A fine summer hotel at the top of the rim rock above the canon, overlooking the valley and presenting one of the grandest views in the Rocky Mountain country should be an investment that would pay a comfortable interest from the start." (Both, courtesy the National Park Service.)

Even though the Grand Valley area is in a borderline desert environment, summer thunderstorms can produce flash floods that can be spectacular to watch but devastating to be near. Occasionally, John Otto's trail work was completely wiped out as flash floods brought large sections of the mountainside over the freshly built trails in the Colorado National Monument or Grand Mesa. (Photograph by Dwight L. Hamilton; courtesy of National Park Service.)

Postcard manufacturer Sanborn produced a packet of photographs of the Colorado National Monument while the Rim Rock Drive was still a graded gravel roadway. A popular daredevil spot for taking pictures was a promontory point appropriately known as Cold Shivers Point on the Trail of the Serpent. (Courtesy of the author's collection.)

Cold Shivers Point on the Trail of the Serpent - Colorado Nat'l. Monument

The names of the monoliths changed often; even a fallen boulder could receive a patriotic name by John Otto: "The big square block of rock detached from the main rim close to the monument shall go by the name of the Altar of Liberty. Further along the rimrock is a monument for Tom Paine; farther on one for Alexander Hamilton. Some people don't like Hamilton, but I'll leave it with—'Who for sheer intellectual grasp and brilliancy stands unrivaled amongst the men of the western half of the world.' Also a monument for Benj. Franklin, Sam Adams, etc. The public is invited to help find the proper names for the different points of interest." (Courtesy of the Western History Department, Denver Public Library.)

In 1909, S. B. Hutchinson of the Grand Junction Chamber of Commerce continued the "boosterism" of the land that would become the Colorado National Monument two years later: "As the end of the trail drew near, the scenery became more interesting, the trail more crooked and rougher to climb, and the views which were obtainable more thrilling and awe-inspiring." (Courtesy of the National Archives and Records Administration, Denver.)

John Otto described the importance of the canyon monoliths: "We are not dealing with a collection of tombstones, but national monuments, bearing the names of our great men, and if ever any entrance portals are constructed at any point of the park's boundary, they should bear the inscription 'Dust thou art, to dust returnest, was not spoken of the soul.' " (Courtesy of the author's collection.)

To the right is Kissing Couple, also called the Fisherman; below, Balanced Rock and a portion of the Fruita Canyon access road are pictured. As John Otto stated: "My aim from the beginning of my work has been to advertise, to make known the Monument Canon Park proposition. Since the proclamation it is forever to be known as 'The Colorado National Monument.' The trails were built to take people into the rim rocks so they would bring back a story. The placing of the pole and raising of the flag helped tell a story." (Both, courtesy of the National Archives and Records Administration, Denver.)

In response to criticism that little was being done to access the park, John Otto explained, "There is only one real true story that goes with the Colorado National Monument, it is the one story without an end. At the beginning of my work it was agreed to name everything out of the United States history as much as possible, leaving out Biblical, foreign, and fictitious names. There is at the east end, on top, 'Liberty Cap,' and at the other end, above Fruita, 'Temple Rock,' carrying the thought God and Liberty. The position of Temple rock to the Washington, the Lincoln monuments, etc. and to the flag on the Independence Monument, readily gives the right impression of the three in order—God, Country, and Flag." (Above, courtesy of the National Archives and Records Administration, Denver; below, courtesy of the author's collection.)

Promotional photographs taken in 1941 reflect John Otto's clarification of his mission: "The Monument park is at the head of this rim-rock country. As stated over and over again, I'm advertising it—I mean, making it known. There is nothing over there to sell, excepting, perhaps, the thousands of cords of dry pinon and cedar. I am not possessed of a trail building mania, nor is it because I have nothing else to do than to write letters to the president of the United States. However, if I hadn't stayed with it, I would never have reached the top of the monument in the canon to place a pole and flag thereon, and, also, if I hadn't stayed with it, the Liberty Cap trail and other trails would have been left for someone else to build." (Both, courtesy of the National Archives and Records Administration, Denver.)

The photograph above shows the Saddlehorn campground. Helping to promote the Colorado National Monument, John Otto paid tribute to the Boy Scouts and Girl Scouts: "I love the boy scouts—girl scouts, too. The story in last nights *Sentinel* tell[ing] that there should be a boy scout movement over in Monument Canon interests me greatly. The whole scenic tract of 14,000 acres should some day become a place of inspiration to the boys and girls of the land. Most all of the monuments have already been named after men out of our own common United States history. A history common enough to be the most interesting of all." (Both, courtesy of the National Archives and Records Administration, Denver.)

Spectacular views of Monument Canyon were promoted by the National Park Service and the Grand Junction Chamber of Commerce. Local youth were recruited to come to the monument for a public relations outing in 1941 to demonstrate the wholesome environment for casual conversation against a background of Praying Hands or Independence Monuments. Or aspiring musicians could enjoy acoustical instruments amid monoliths that include the Organ Pipes in Monument Canyon. Photographs were circulated to newspapers, railroad publications, and other travel magazines throughout the world to promote the national monument. (Both, courtesy of the National Archives and Records Administration, Denver.)

Coordinating superintendent John S. McLaughlin described the national significance of the Colorado National Monument in a 1940s memorandum: "This national monument contains unusual geological features and splendid examples of massively eroded, colorful sandstone. Fascinating canyons and rock forms have been carved through this massive cap rock, chiefly by the action of wind, water, and temperature changes over long periods of time. . . . An excellent highway known as the Rim Rock Drive traverses most of the monument. Few visitors can travel this drive without deriving a feeling of exhilaration from the wide panoramas which it commands, and a desire to know more about the natural forces that caused it all." (Both, courtesy of the National Archives and Records Administration, Denver.)

As an 1883 editorial in the *Grand Junction News* predicted, "No road can be built in Mesa county which shall answer a just demand that does not begin or end at Grand Junction. Nine-tenths of all the actual property and business of the county centre here, and all the interests of the county centre here. Every out-lying district should be accommodated as soon as it is practicable, but not to the extent of incurring heavy expense when there is nothing to warrant it." (Both, courtesy of the National Archives and Records Administration, Denver.)

John Otto predicted the future for the region in 1912 and the need to build a national park–to–national park highway that would enable tourists to visit all the national parks on one cross-country highway: "From the Grand mesa to the Grand canon, from the Grand valley to the sea, 'that's my territory.' Only the dreams that come true are the ones worth dreaming. About a 700-mile dream will take us from the Grand valley at the foot of Grand mesa to the sea by way of the Grand canon, some day a reality by road." (Above, courtesy of the National Archives and Records Administration; below, courtesy of the Western History Collection, Denver Public Library.)

EPILOGUE

While researching any historic project, it is always rewarding when an obscure piece of information is found. This was a memorandum issued during World War II:

February 12, 1942

MEMORANDUM for the Custodian, Colorado National Monument

In order to conserve paper for the duration of the emergency, it is requested that you discontinue the practice of forwarding memorandums to this office in duplicate, and forward one copy only.

If additional copies are needed, we will make them here. This, of course, does not apply to your monthly narrative report or to any other report which you know requires a stated number of copies.

However, it is noted that you are sending your monthly narrative in eight copies, whereas only <u>seven</u> are required. The monthly travel report should be sent in <u>eight</u> copies, as previously requested.

John S. McLaughlin
Coordinating Superintendent

DISCOVER THOUSANDS OF LOCAL HISTORY BOOKS FEATURING MILLIONS OF VINTAGE IMAGES

Arcadia Publishing, the leading local history publisher in the United States, is committed to making history accessible and meaningful through publishing books that celebrate and preserve the heritage of America's people and places.

Find more books like this at
www.arcadiapublishing.com

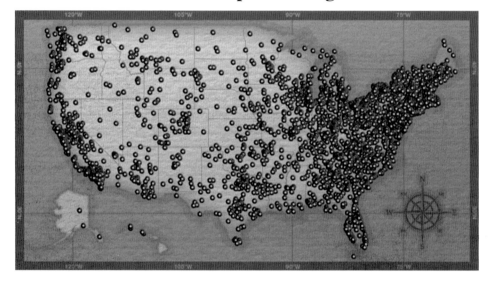

Search for your hometown history, your old stomping grounds, and even your favorite sports team.